PAPERBACK ISBN: 978-1-955605-45-8
HARDBACK ISBN: 978-1-955605-46-5

Cover and Interior Design: B.O.Y. Enterprises, Inc.

Printed in the United States.

Hello There!

Name:_____

Is Ready for a Work/ Life Harmony

"I am capable, I am strong If I believe in myself, I can turn my dreams into a plan, and my plan into my reality."
Shelly Brown Y.

WWW.2P/LLC.COM

The Work/Life Harmony
Planner

was created for aspiring entrepreneurs who are trying to figure out where to start and how to find the balance between starting a business and maintaining a happy home.

This planner has everything at your fingertips, so all you have to do is write it down, track, and manage the process. Everything from doctors' appointments, quotes, notes, and social media posts, to points of contact is, even how often you are working out.

This comprehensive planner will guide you and help you create a unique and customized roadmap so your home and business will be successful. The Work/Life planner is for aspiring entrepreneurs who are driven, ambitious, creative, and determined to build a business and life they love.

In health & happiness,

Vernita Stevens

"Finally, my brethren, be strong in the Lord and in the power of His might." -Ephesians 6:10 NKJV

2024

JANUARY

S	M	T	W	T	F	S
	1	2	3	4	5	6
7	8	9	10	11	12	13
14	15	16	17	18	19	20
21	22	23	24	25	26	27
28	29	30	31			

FEBRUARY

S	M	T	W	T	F	S
				1	2	3
4	5	6	7	8	9	10
11	12	13	14	15	16	17
18	19	20	21	22	23	24
25	26	27	28	29		

MARCH

S	M	T	W	T	F	S
					1	2
3	4	5	6	7	8	9
10	11	12	13	14	15	16
17	18	19	20	21	22	23
24	25	26	27	28	29	30
31						

APRIL

S	M	T	W	T	F	S
	1	2	3	4	5	6
7	8	9	10	11	12	13
14	15	16	17	18	19	20
21	22	23	24	25	26	27
28	29	30				

MAY

S	M	T	W	T	F	S
			1	2	3	4
5	6	7	8	9	10	11
12	13	14	15	16	17	18
19	20	21	22	23	24	25
26	27	28	29	30	31	

JUNE

S	M	T	W	T	F	S
						1
2	3	4	5	6	7	8
9	10	11	12	13	14	15
16	17	18	19	20	21	22
23	24	25	26	27	28	29
30						

JULY

S	M	T	W	T	F	S
	1	2	3	4	5	6
7	8	9	10	11	12	13
14	15	16	17	18	19	20
21	22	23	24	25	26	27
28	29	30	31			

AUGUST

S	M	T	W	T	F	S
				1	2	3
4	5	6	7	8	9	10
11	12	13	14	15	16	17
18	19	20	21	22	23	24
25	26	27	28	29	30	31

SEPTEMBER

S	M	T	W	T	F	S
1	2	3	4	5	6	7
8	9	10	11	12	13	14
15	16	17	18	19	20	21
22	23	24	25	26	27	28
29	30					

OCTOBER

S	M	T	W	T	F	S
		1	2	3	4	5
6	7	8	9	10	11	12
13	14	15	16	17	18	19
20	21	22	23	24	25	26
27	28	29	30	31		

NOVEMBER

S	M	T	W	T	F	S
					1	2
3	4	5	6	7	8	9
10	11	12	13	14	15	16
17	18	19	20	21	22	23
24	25	26	27	28	29	30

DECEMBER

S	M	T	W	T	F	S
1	2	3	4	5	6	7
8	9	10	11	12	13	14
15	16	17	18	19	20	21
22	23	24	25	26	27	28
29	30	31				

2025

JANUARY

S	M	T	W	T	F	S
			1	2	3	4
5	6	7	8	9	10	11
12	13	14	15	16	17	18
19	20	21	22	23	24	25
26	27	28	29	30	31	

FEBRUARY

S	M	T	W	T	F	S
						1
2	3	4	5	6	7	8
9	10	11	12	13	14	15
16	17	18	19	20	21	22
23	24	25	26	27	28	

MARCH

S	M	T	W	T	F	S
						1
2	3	4	5	6	7	8
9	10	11	12	13	14	15
16	17	18	19	20	21	22
23	24	25	26	27	28	29
30	31					

APRIL

S	M	T	W	T	F	S
		1	2	3	4	5
6	7	8	9	10	11	12
13	14	15	16	17	18	19
20	21	22	23	24	25	26
27	28	29	30			

MAY

S	M	T	W	T	F	S
				1	2	3
4	5	6	7	8	9	10
11	12	13	14	15	16	17
18	19	20	21	22	23	24
25	26	27	28	29	30	31

JUNE

S	M	T	W	T	F	S
1	2	3	4	5	6	7
8	9	10	11	12	13	14
15	16	17	18	19	20	21
22	23	24	25	26	27	28
29	30					

JULY

S	M	T	W	T	F	S
		1	2	3	4	5
6	7	8	9	10	11	12
13	14	15	16	17	18	19
20	21	22	23	24	25	26
27	28	29	30	31		

AUGUST

S	M	T	W	T	F	S
					1	2
3	4	5	6	7	8	9
10	11	12	13	14	15	16
17	18	19	20	21	22	23
24	25	26	27	28	29	30
31						

SEPTEMBER

S	M	T	W	T	F	S
	1	2	3	4	5	6
7	8	9	10	11	12	13
14	15	16	17	18	19	20
21	22	23	24	25	26	27
28	29	30				

OCTOBER

S	M	T	W	T	F	S
			1	2	3	4
5	6	7	8	9	10	11
12	13	14	15	16	17	18
19	20	21	22	23	24	25
26	27	28	29	30	31	

NOVEMBER

S	M	T	W	T	F	S
						1
2	3	4	5	6	7	8
9	10	11	12	13	14	15
16	17	18	19	20	21	22
23	24	25	26	27	28	29
30						

DECEMBER

S	M	T	W	T	F	S
	1	2	3	4	5	6
7	8	9	10	11	12	13
14	15	16	17	18	19	20
21	22	23	24	25	26	27
28	29	30	31			

MONTH-*at-a-glance*
PLANNER

MONTH:

Mon	Tues	Wed	Thur	Fri	Sat	Sun

NOTES

"We need to do a better job of putting ourselves higher on our own "To Do List". - **Michelle Obama**

MONTHLY *expenses*

Month:_____

RECURRING EXPENSES

Software, Memberships, Household bills etc.	Amount
TOTAL RECURRING EXPENSES	$

VARIABLE EXPENSES

Contractors, Supplies, etc.	Amount
TOTAL VARIABLE EXPENSES	$
TOTAL MONTHLY EXPENSES	$

DATE:

weekly
GOALS

personal

○

○

○

○

top priorities

☐ _____

☐ _____

☐ _____

professional

○

○

○

○

top priorities

☐ _____

☐ _____

☐ _____

spiritual

○

○

○

○

top priorities

☐ _____

☐ _____

☐ _____

Habit Tracker

List any patterns to monitor & track good or bad habits to find work/life harmony

SUNDAY _____

MONDAY _____

TUESDAY _____

WEDNESDAY _____

THURSDAY _____

FRIDAY _____

SATURDAY _____

FITNESS TRACKER (STAY ACTIVE- EXERCISE AT LEAST 3 TIMES A WEEK, MAKE HEALTHY CHOICES, DRINK WATER

DAY	ACTIVITY	DURATION	H20
SUNDAY			
MONDAY			
TUESDAY			
WEDNESDAY			
THURSDAY			
FRIDAY			
SATURDAY			

Week of: _____ Weekly To-Do's

Monday

Tuesday

Wednesday

Thursday

Friday

Saturday & Sunday

Weekly
Inspirational Thought

_____
_____
_____
_____
_____
_____
_____
_____

Weekly
Prayer Devotion

_____
_____
_____
_____
_____

This Week's Wins:

What goals need improvement?

Notes

_____
_____
_____
_____
_____
_____
_____
_____
_____
_____
_____

DATE: _____

weekly
GOALS

personal

- ○
- ○
- ○
- ○

top priorities

- ☐
- ☐
- ☐

professional

- ○
- ○
- ○
- ○

top priorities

- ☐
- ☐
- ☐

spiritual

- ○
- ○
- ○
- ○

top priorities

- ☐
- ☐
- ☐

Habit Tracker

List any patterns to monitor & track good or bad habits to find work/life harmony

SUNDAY _____

MONDAY_____

TUESDAY_____

WEDNESDAY_____

THURSDAY_____

FRIDAY_____

SATURDAY_____

FITNESS TRACKER (STAY ACTIVE- EXERCISE AT LEAST 3 TIMES A WEEK, MAKE HEALTHY CHOICES, DRINK WATER

DAY	ACTIVITY	DURATION	H20
SUNDAY			
MONDAY			
TUESDAY			
WEDNESDAY			
THURSDAY			
FRIDAY			
SATURDAY			

Week of: _____ Weekly To-Do's

Monday

Tuesday

Wednesday

Thursday

Friday

Saturday & Sunday

Weekly
Inspirational Thought

_____
_____
_____
_____
_____
_____
_____
_____
_____

Weekly
Prayer Devotion

_____
_____
_____
_____
_____

This Week's Wins:

- ○
- ○
- ○
- ○

Notes

_____
_____
_____
_____
_____
_____
_____
_____
_____
_____
_____
_____

What goals need improvement?

- ○
- ○
- ○
- ○

DATE:

weekly
GOALS

personal

- ○
- ○
- ○
- ○

top priorities

- [ ]
- [ ]
- [ ]

professional

- ○
- ○
- ○
- ○

top priorities

- [ ]
- [ ]
- [ ]

spiritual

- ○
- ○
- ○
- ○

top priorities

- [ ]
- [ ]
- [ ]

Habit Tracker

List any patterns to monitor & track good or bad habits to find work/life harmony

SUNDAY _____

MONDAY_____

TUESDAY_____

WEDNESDAY_____

THURSDAY_____

FRIDAY_____

SATURDAY_____

FITNESS TRACKER (STAY ACTIVE- EXERCISE AT LEAST 3 TIMES A WEEK, MAKE HEALTHY CHOICES, DRINK WATER

DAY	ACTIVITY	DURATION	H20
SUNDAY			
MONDAY			
TUESDAY			
WEDNESDAY			
THURSDAY			
FRIDAY			
SATURDAY			

Week of: _____ Weekly To-Do's

Monday

Tuesday

Wednesday

Thursday

Friday

Saturday & Sunday

Weekly
Inspirational Thought

_____
_____
_____
_____
_____
_____
_____

Notes

_____
_____
_____
_____
_____
_____
_____
_____
_____
_____
_____
_____

Weekly
Prayer Devotion

_____
_____
_____
_____
_____

This Week's Wins:

What goals need improvement?

weekly
GOALS

personal

○

○

○

○

top priorities

☐

☐

☐

professional

○

○

○

○

top priorities

☐

☐

☐

spiritual

○

○

○

○

top priorities

☐

☐

☐

Habit Tracker

List any patterns to monitor & track good or bad habits to find work/life harmony

SUNDAY _____

MONDAY _____

TUESDAY _____

WEDNESDAY _____

THURSDAY _____

FRIDAY _____

SATURDAY _____

FITNESS TRACKER (STAY ACTIVE- EXERCISE AT LEAST 3 TIMES A WEEK, MAKE HEALTHY CHOICES, DRINK WATER

DAY	ACTIVITY	DURATION	H20
SUNDAY			
MONDAY			
TUESDAY			
WEDNESDAY			
THURSDAY			
FRIDAY			
SATURDAY			

Week of: _____ Weekly To-Do's

Monday

Tuesday

Wednesday

Thursday

Friday

Saturday & Sunday

Weekly
Inspirational Thought

_____
_____
_____
_____
_____
_____
_____
_____

Weekly
Prayer Devotion

_____
_____
_____
_____
_____

This Week's Wins:

- ◯
- ◯
- ◯
- ◯

What goals need improvement?

- ◯
- ◯
- ◯
- ◯

Notes

_____
_____
_____
_____
_____
_____
_____
_____
_____
_____

MONTHLY SOCIAL MEDIA PLAN

Posting Dates

THEMES OF THE MONTH

- [ ]
- [ ]
- [ ]
- [ ]
- [ ]

BRAINSTORM POST TOPICS

_____
_____
_____
_____
_____
_____
_____
_____
_____
_____

HASHTAGS/KEYWORDS

_____
_____
_____
_____
_____
_____

NOTES

Monthly Review

Family Time: (dinner, board games, activities, etc)

_____

_____

Maintenance Website/Update Apps:

_____

_____

Balance Financial Books

_____

_____

Cancel and/or Update Subscriptions:

_____

_____

Other:

_____

_____

MONTH-*at-a-glance*
PLANNER

MONTH:

Mon	Tues	Wed	Thur	Fri	Sat	Sun

NOTES

_____

_____

_____

_____

_____

"The challenge of work-life balance is without question one of the most significant struggles faced by modern man." -**Stephen Covey**

MONTHLY *expenses*

Month:_____

RECURRING EXPENSES

Software, Memberships, Household bills etc.	Amount
TOTAL RECURRING EXPENSES	$

VARIABLE EXPENSES

Contractors, Supplies, etc.	Amount
TOTAL VARIABLE EXPENSES	$
TOTAL MONTHLY EXPENSES	$

DATE:

weekly
GOALS

personal

○

○

○

○

top priorities

☐

☐

☐

professional

○

○

○

○

top priorities

☐

☐

☐

spiritual

○

○

○

○

top priorities

☐

☐

☐

Habit Tracker

List any patterns to monitor & track good or bad habits to find work/life harmony

SUNDAY _____

MONDAY_____

TUESDAY_____

WEDNESDAY_____

THURSDAY_____

FRIDAY_____

SATURDAY_____

FITNESS TRACKER (STAY ACTIVE- EXERCISE AT LEAST 3 TIMES A WEEK, MAKE HEALTHY CHOICES, DRINK WATER

DAY	ACTIVITY	DURATION	H20
SUNDAY			
MONDAY			
TUESDAY			
WEDNESDAY			
THURSDAY			
FRIDAY			
SATURDAY			

Week of: _____ Weekly To-Do's

Monday

Tuesday

Wednesday

Thursday

Friday

Saturday & Sunday

Weekly
Inspirational Thought

_____
_____
_____
_____
_____
_____
_____
_____

Weekly
Prayer Devotion

_____
_____
_____
_____
_____

This Week's Wins:

- ○
- ○
- ○
- ○

What goals need improvement?

- ○
- ○
- ○
- ○

Notes

_____
_____
_____
_____
_____
_____
_____
_____
_____
_____
_____

weekly
GOALS

personal

○
○
○
○

top priorities

☐
☐
☐

professional

○
○
○
○

top priorities

☐
☐
☐

spiritual

○
○
○
○

top priorities

☐
☐
☐

Habit Tracker

List any patterns to monitor & track good or bad habits to find work/life harmony

SUNDAY _____

MONDAY _____

TUESDAY _____

WEDNESDAY _____

THURSDAY _____

FRIDAY _____

SATURDAY _____

FITNESS TRACKER (STAY ACTIVE- EXERCISE AT LEAST 3 TIMES A WEEK, MAKE HEALTHY CHOICES, DRINK WATER

DAY	ACTIVITY	DURATION	H20
SUNDAY			
MONDAY			
TUESDAY			
WEDNESDAY			
THURSDAY			
FRIDAY			
SATURDAY			

Week of: _____ Weekly To-Do's

Monday

Tuesday

Wednesday

Thursday

Friday

Saturday & Sunday

Weekly
Inspirational Thought

_____
_____
_____
_____
_____
_____
_____
_____

Weekly
Prayer Devotion

_____
_____
_____
_____
_____

This Week's Wins:

Notes

_____
_____
_____
_____
_____
_____
_____
_____
_____
_____
_____
_____

What goals need improvement?

weekly
GOALS

personal

○

○

○

○

top priorities

☐

☐

☐

professional

○

○

○

○

top priorities

☐

☐

☐

spiritual

○

○

○

○

top priorities

☐

☐

☐

Habit Tracker

List any patterns to monitor & track good or bad habits to find work/life harmony

SUNDAY _____

MONDAY _____

TUESDAY _____

WEDNESDAY _____

THURSDAY _____

FRIDAY _____

SATURDAY _____

FITNESS TRACKER (STAY ACTIVE- EXERCISE AT LEAST 3 TIMES A
WEEK, MAKE HEALTHY CHOICES, DRINK WATER

DAY	ACTIVITY	DURATION	H20
SUNDAY			
MONDAY			
TUESDAY			
WEDNESDAY			
THURSDAY			
FRIDAY			
SATURDAY			

Week of: _____ Weekly To-Do's

Monday

Tuesday

Wednesday

Thursday

Friday

Saturday & Sunday

Weekly
Inspirational Thought

_____
_____
_____
_____
_____
_____
_____
_____

Notes

_____
_____
_____
_____
_____
_____
_____
_____
_____
_____
_____

Weekly
Prayer Devotion

_____
_____
_____
_____
_____

This Week's Wins:

What goals need improvement?

DATE:

weekly
GOALS

personal

- ○
- ○
- ○
- ○

top priorities

- ☐
- ☐
- ☐

professional

- ○
- ○
- ○
- ○

top priorities

- ☐
- ☐
- ☐

spiritual

- ○
- ○
- ○
- ○

top priorities

- ☐
- ☐
- ☐

Habit Tracker

List any patterns to monitor & track good or bad habits to find work/life harmony

SUNDAY _____

MONDAY _____

TUESDAY _____

WEDNESDAY _____

THURSDAY _____

FRIDAY _____

SATURDAY _____

FITNESS TRACKER (STAY ACTIVE- EXERCISE AT LEAST 3 TIMES A WEEK, MAKE HEALTHY CHOICES, DRINK WATER

DAY	ACTIVITY	DURATION	H20
SUNDAY			
MONDAY			
TUESDAY			
WEDNESDAY			
THURSDAY			
FRIDAY			
SATURDAY			

Week of: _____ Weekly To-Do's

Monday

Tuesday

Wednesday

Thursday

Friday

Saturday & Sunday

Weekly
Inspirational Thought

_____
_____
_____
_____
_____
_____
_____
_____

Weekly
Prayer Devotion

_____
_____
_____
_____
_____

This Week's Wins:

- ○
- ○
- ○
- ○

Notes

_____
_____
_____
_____
_____
_____
_____
_____
_____
_____
_____
_____

What goals need improvement?

- ○
- ○
- ○
- ○

MONTHLY SOCIAL MEDIA PLAN

THEMES OF THE MONTH

- [ ]
- [ ]
- [ ]
- [ ]
- [ ]

BRAINSTORM POST TOPICS

Posting Dates

Instagram	
Facebook	
Pinterest	
YouTube	
LinkedIn	

HASHTAGS/KEYWORDS

NOTES

Monthly
Review

Family Time: (dinner, board games, activities, etc)

_____

_____

Maintenance Website/Update Apps:

_____

_____

Balance Financial Books

_____

_____

Cancel and/or Update Subscriptions:

_____

_____

Other:

_____

_____

MONTH-*at-a-glance* PLANNER

MONTH:

Mon	Tues	Wed	Thur	Fri	Sat	Sun

NOTES

_____

_____

_____

_____

_____

"Everyone wants to live on top of the mountain, but all the happiness and growth occurs while you're climbing it." -**Stephen Covey**

MONTHLY *expenses*

Month:_____

RECURRING EXPENSES

Software, Memberships, Household bills etc.	Amount
TOTAL RECURRING EXPENSES	$

VARIABLE EXPENSES

Contractors, Supplies, etc.	Amount
TOTAL VARIABLE EXPENSES	$
TOTAL MONTHLY EXPENSES	$

weekly
GOALS

personal

- ○
- ○
- ○
- ○

top priorities

- ☐
- ☐
- ☐

professional

- ○
- ○
- ○
- ○

top priorities

- ☐
- ☐
- ☐

spiritual

- ○
- ○
- ○
- ○

top priorities

- ☐
- ☐
- ☐

Habit Tracker

List any patterns to monitor & track good or bad habits to find work/life harmony

SUNDAY _____

MONDAY_____

TUESDAY_____

WEDNESDAY_____

THURSDAY_____

FRIDAY_____

SATURDAY_____

FITNESS TRACKER (STAY ACTIVE- EXERCISE AT LEAST 3 TIMES A WEEK, MAKE HEALTHY CHOICES, DRINK WATER

DAY	ACTIVITY	DURATION	H20
SUNDAY			
MONDAY			
TUESDAY			
WEDNESDAY			
THURSDAY			
FRIDAY			
SATURDAY			

Week of: _____ Weekly To-Do's

Monday

Tuesday

Wednesday

Thursday

Friday

Saturday & Sunday

Weekly
Inspirational Thought

_____
_____
_____
_____
_____
_____
_____

Notes

_____
_____
_____
_____
_____
_____
_____
_____
_____
_____
_____

Weekly
Prayer Devotion

_____
_____
_____
_____
_____

This Week's Wins:

- ◯
- ◯
- ◯
- ◯

What goals need improvement?

- ◯
- ◯
- ◯
- ◯

DATE:

weekly
GOALS

personal

- ○
- ○
- ○
- ○

top priorities

- ☐
- ☐
- ☐

professional

- ○
- ○
- ○
- ○

top priorities

- ☐
- ☐
- ☐

spiritual

- ○
- ○
- ○
- ○

top priorities

- ☐
- ☐
- ☐

Habit Tracker

List any patterns to monitor & track good or bad habits to find work/life harmony

SUNDAY _____

MONDAY _____

TUESDAY _____

WEDNESDAY _____

THURSDAY _____

FRIDAY _____

SATURDAY _____

FITNESS TRACKER (STAY ACTIVE- EXERCISE AT LEAST 3 TIMES A WEEK, MAKE HEALTHY CHOICES, DRINK WATER

DAY	ACTIVITY	DURATION	H20
SUNDAY			
MONDAY			
TUESDAY			
WEDNESDAY			
THURSDAY			
FRIDAY			
SATURDAY			

Week of: _____ Weekly To-Do's

Monday

Tuesday

Wednesday

Thursday

Friday

Saturday & Sunday

Weekly
Inspirational Thought

_____
_____
_____
_____
_____
_____
_____
_____
_____

Weekly
Prayer Devotion

_____
_____
_____
_____
_____

This Week's Wins:

Notes

_____
_____
_____
_____
_____
_____
_____
_____
_____
_____
_____
_____

What goals need improvement?

DATE:

weekly
GOALS

personal

- ○
- ○
- ○
- ○

top priorities

- ☐
- ☐
- ☐

professional

- ○
- ○
- ○
- ○

top priorities

- ☐
- ☐
- ☐

spiritual

- ○
- ○
- ○
- ○

top priorities

- ☐
- ☐
- ☐

Habit Tracker

List any patterns to monitor & track good or bad habits to find work/life harmony

SUNDAY _____

MONDAY _____

TUESDAY _____

WEDNESDAY _____

THURSDAY _____

FRIDAY _____

SATURDAY _____

FITNESS TRACKER (STAY ACTIVE- EXERCISE AT LEAST 3 TIMES A WEEK, MAKE HEALTHY CHOICES, DRINK WATER

DAY	ACTIVITY	DURATION	H20
SUNDAY			
MONDAY			
TUESDAY			
WEDNESDAY			
THURSDAY			
FRIDAY			
SATURDAY			

Week of: _____ Weekly To-Do's

Monday

Tuesday

Wednesday

Thursday

Friday

Saturday & Sunday

Weekly
Inspirational Thought

_____
_____
_____
_____
_____
_____
_____
_____

Weekly
Prayer Devotion

_____
_____
_____
_____
_____

This Week's Wins:

- ○
- ○
- ○
- ○

What goals need improvement?

- ○
- ○
- ○
- ○

Notes

_____
_____
_____
_____
_____
_____
_____
_____
_____
_____
_____
_____

DATE:

weekly
GOALS

personal

- ○
- ○
- ○
- ○

top priorities

- ☐
- ☐
- ☐

professional

- ○
- ○
- ○
- ○

top priorities

- ☐
- ☐
- ☐

spiritual

- ○
- ○
- ○
- ○

top priorities

- ☐
- ☐
- ☐

Habit Tracker

List any patterns to monitor & track good or bad habits to find work/life harmony

SUNDAY _____

MONDAY _____

TUESDAY _____

WEDNESDAY _____

THURSDAY _____

FRIDAY _____

SATURDAY _____

FITNESS TRACKER (STAY ACTIVE- EXERCISE AT LEAST 3 TIMES A WEEK, MAKE HEALTHY CHOICES, DRINK WATER

DAY	ACTIVITY	DURATION	H20
SUNDAY			
MONDAY			
TUESDAY			
WEDNESDAY			
THURSDAY			
FRIDAY			
SATURDAY			

Week of: _____ Weekly To-Do's

Monday

Tuesday

Wednesday

Thursday

Friday

Saturday & Sunday

Weekly
Inspirational Thought

_____

_____

_____

_____

_____

_____

_____

_____

Weekly
Prayer Devotion

_____

_____

_____

_____

_____

This Week's Wins:

Notes

_____

_____

_____

_____

_____

_____

_____

_____

_____

_____

_____

_____

What goals need improvement?

MONTHLY SOCIAL MEDIA PLAN

THEMES OF THE MONTH

- [ ]
- [ ]
- [ ]
- [ ]
- [ ]

BRAINSTORM POST TOPICS

_____
_____
_____
_____
_____
_____
_____
_____
_____

Posting Dates

Instagram	
Facebook	
Pinterest	
YouTube	
LinkedIn	

HASHTAGS/KEYWORDS

_____
_____
_____
_____
_____
_____

NOTES

Monthly Review

Family Time: (dinner, board games, activities, etc)

_____

_____

Maintenance Website/Update Apps:

_____

_____

Balance Financial Books

_____

_____

Cancel and/or Update Subscriptions:

_____

_____

Other:

_____

_____

MONTH-*at-a-glance*
PLANNER

MONTH:

Mon	Tues	Wed	Thur	Fri	Sat	Sun

NOTES

_____

_____

_____

"Balance: Never let success go to your head. Never let failure go to your heart." -**Unknown**

_____

MONTHLY *expenses*

Month:_____

RECURRING EXPENSES

Software, Memberships, Household bills etc.	Amount
TOTAL RECURRING EXPENSES	$

VARIABLE EXPENSES

Contractors, Supplies, etc.	Amount
TOTAL VARIABLE EXPENSES	$
TOTAL MONTHLY EXPENSES	$

weekly
GOALS

personal

- ○
- ○
- ○
- ○

top priorities

- ☐
- ☐
- ☐

professional

- ○
- ○
- ○
- ○

top priorities

- ☐
- ☐
- ☐

spiritual

- ○
- ○
- ○
- ○

top priorities

- ☐
- ☐
- ☐

Habit Tracker

List any patterns to monitor & track good or bad habits to find work/life harmony

SUNDAY _____

MONDAY _____

TUESDAY _____

WEDNESDAY _____

THURSDAY _____

FRIDAY _____

SATURDAY _____

FITNESS TRACKER (STAY ACTIVE- EXERCISE AT LEAST 3 TIMES A WEEK, MAKE HEALTHY CHOICES, DRINK WATER

DAY	ACTIVITY	DURATION	H20
SUNDAY			
MONDAY			
TUESDAY			
WEDNESDAY			
THURSDAY			
FRIDAY			
SATURDAY			

Week of: _____ Weekly To-Do's

Monday

Tuesday

Wednesday

Thursday

Friday

Saturday & Sunday

Weekly
Inspirational Thought

_____
_____
_____
_____
_____
_____
_____
_____

Weekly
Prayer Devotion

_____
_____
_____
_____
_____

This Week's Wins:

- ◯
- ◯
- ◯
- ◯

Notes

_____
_____
_____
_____
_____
_____
_____
_____
_____
_____
_____

What goals need improvement?

- ◯
- ◯
- ◯
- ◯

weekly
GOALS

personal

- ○
- ○
- ○
- ○

top priorities

- ☐
- ☐
- ☐

professional

- ○
- ○
- ○
- ○

top priorities

- ☐
- ☐
- ☐

spiritual

- ○
- ○
- ○
- ○

top priorities

- ☐
- ☐
- ☐

Habit Tracker

List any patterns to monitor & track good or bad habits to find work/life harmony

SUNDAY _____

MONDAY _____

TUESDAY _____

WEDNESDAY _____

THURSDAY _____

FRIDAY _____

SATURDAY _____

FITNESS TRACKER (STAY ACTIVE- EXERCISE AT LEAST 3 TIMES A WEEK, MAKE HEALTHY CHOICES, DRINK WATER

DAY	ACTIVITY	DURATION	H20
SUNDAY			
MONDAY			
TUESDAY			
WEDNESDAY			
THURSDAY			
FRIDAY			
SATURDAY			

Week of: _____ Weekly To-Do's

Monday

Tuesday

Wednesday

Thursday

Friday

Saturday & Sunday

Weekly
Inspirational Thought

_____
_____
_____
_____
_____
_____
_____
_____

Weekly
Prayer Devotion

_____
_____
_____
_____
_____

This Week's Wins:

Notes

_____
_____
_____
_____
_____
_____
_____
_____
_____
_____
_____
_____
_____

What goals need improvement?

weekly
GOALS

personal

- ○
- ○
- ○
- ○

top priorities

- ☐
- ☐
- ☐

professional

- ○
- ○
- ○
- ○

top priorities

- ☐
- ☐
- ☐

spiritual

- ○
- ○
- ○
- ○

top priorities

- ☐
- ☐
- ☐

Habit Tracker

List any patterns to monitor & track good or bad habits to find work/life harmony

SUNDAY _____

MONDAY _____

TUESDAY _____

WEDNESDAY _____

THURSDAY _____

FRIDAY _____

SATURDAY _____

FITNESS TRACKER (STAY ACTIVE- EXERCISE AT LEAST 3 TIMES A WEEK, MAKE HEALTHY CHOICES, DRINK WATER

DAY	ACTIVITY	DURATION	H20
SUNDAY			
MONDAY			
TUESDAY			
WEDNESDAY			
THURSDAY			
FRIDAY			
SATURDAY			

Week of: _____ Weekly To-Do's

Monday

Tuesday

Wednesday

Thursday

Friday

Saturday & Sunday

Weekly
Inspirational Thought

_____
_____
_____
_____
_____
_____
_____
_____

Notes

_____
_____
_____
_____
_____
_____
_____
_____
_____
_____
_____
_____
_____

Weekly
Prayer Devotion

_____
_____
_____
_____
_____

This Week's Wins:

- ◯
- ◯
- ◯
- ◯

What goals need improvement?

- ◯
- ◯
- ◯
- ◯

weekly
GOALS

personal

- ○
- ○
- ○
- ○

top priorities

- ☐
- ☐
- ☐

professional

- ○
- ○
- ○
- ○

top priorities

- ☐
- ☐
- ☐

spiritual

- ○
- ○
- ○
- ○

top priorities

- ☐
- ☐
- ☐

Habit Tracker

List any patterns to monitor & track good or bad habits to find work/life harmony

SUNDAY _____

MONDAY _____

TUESDAY _____

WEDNESDAY _____

THURSDAY _____

FRIDAY _____

SATURDAY _____

FITNESS TRACKER (STAY ACTIVE- EXERCISE AT LEAST 3 TIMES A WEEK, MAKE HEALTHY CHOICES, DRINK WATER

DAY	ACTIVITY	DURATION	H20
SUNDAY			
MONDAY			
TUESDAY			
WEDNESDAY			
THURSDAY			
FRIDAY			
SATURDAY			

Week of: _____ Weekly To-Do's

Monday

Tuesday

Wednesday

Thursday

Friday

Saturday & Sunday

Weekly
Inspirational Thought

_____
_____
_____
_____
_____
_____
_____
_____

Weekly
Prayer Devotion

_____
_____
_____
_____
_____

This Week's Wins:

- ◯
- ◯
- ◯
- ◯

Notes

_____
_____
_____
_____
_____
_____
_____
_____
_____
_____
_____
_____

What goals need improvement?

- ◯
- ◯
- ◯
- ◯

MONTHLY SOCIAL MEDIA PLAN

THEMES OF THE MONTH

- [ ]
- [ ]
- [ ]
- [ ]
- [ ]

BRAINSTORM POST TOPICS

_____
_____
_____
_____
_____
_____
_____
_____
_____
_____

Posting Dates

Instagram	
Facebook	
Pinterest	
YouTube	
LinkedIn	

HASHTAGS/KEYWORDS

_____
_____
_____
_____
_____
_____

NOTES

Monthly Review

Family Time: (dinner, board games, activities, etc)

_____

_____

Maintenance Website/Update Apps:

_____

_____

Balance Financial Books

_____

_____

Cancel and/or Update Subscriptions:

_____

_____

Other:

_____

_____

MONTH-*at-a-glance* PLANNER

MONTH:

Mon	Tues	Wed	Thur	Fri	Sat	Sun

NOTES

_____

_____

_____   *"Your best teacher is your last mistake."*

_____   **-Ralph Nader**

_____

MONTHLY *expenses*

Month:_____

RECURRING EXPENSES

Software, Memberships, Household bills etc.	Amount
TOTAL RECURRING EXPENSES	$

VARIABLE EXPENSES

Contractors, Supplies, etc.	Amount
TOTAL VARIABLE EXPENSES	$
TOTAL MONTHLY EXPENSES	$

weekly
GOALS

personal

○

○

○

○

top priorities

☐

☐

☐

professional

○

○

○

○

top priorities

☐

☐

☐

spiritual

○

○

○

○

top priorities

☐

☐

☐

Habit Tracker

List any patterns to monitor & track good or bad habits to find work/life harmony

SUNDAY _____

MONDAY _____

TUESDAY _____

WEDNESDAY _____

THURSDAY _____

FRIDAY _____

SATURDAY _____

FITNESS TRACKER (STAY ACTIVE- EXERCISE AT LEAST 3 TIMES A WEEK, MAKE HEALTHY CHOICES, DRINK WATER

DAY	ACTIVITY	DURATION	H20
SUNDAY			
MONDAY			
TUESDAY			
WEDNESDAY			
THURSDAY			
FRIDAY			
SATURDAY			

Week of: _____ Weekly To-Do's

Monday

Tuesday

Wednesday

Thursday

Friday

Saturday & Sunday

Weekly
Inspirational Thought

_____
_____
_____
_____
_____
_____
_____
_____

Weekly
Prayer Devotion

_____
_____
_____
_____
_____

This Week's Wins:

Notes

_____
_____
_____
_____
_____
_____
_____
_____
_____
_____
_____

What goals need improvement?

DATE:

weekly
GOALS

personal

- ○
- ○
- ○
- ○

top priorities

- ☐
- ☐
- ☐

professional

- ○
- ○
- ○
- ○

top priorities

- ☐
- ☐
- ☐

spiritual

- ○
- ○
- ○
- ○

top priorities

- ☐
- ☐
- ☐

Habit Tracker

List any patterns to monitor & track good or bad habits to find work/life harmony

SUNDAY _____

MONDAY _____

TUESDAY _____

WEDNESDAY _____

THURSDAY _____

FRIDAY _____

SATURDAY _____

FITNESS TRACKER (STAY ACTIVE- EXERCISE AT LEAST 3 TIMES A WEEK, MAKE HEALTHY CHOICES, DRINK WATER

DAY	ACTIVITY	DURATION	H20
SUNDAY			
MONDAY			
TUESDAY			
WEDNESDAY			
THURSDAY			
FRIDAY			
SATURDAY			

Week of: _____ Weekly To-Do's

Monday

Tuesday

Wednesday

Thursday

Friday

Saturday & Sunday

Weekly
Inspirational Thought

_____

_____

_____

_____

_____

_____

_____

Weekly
Prayer Devotion

_____

_____

_____

_____

_____

This Week's Wins:

Notes

_____

_____

_____

_____

_____

_____

_____

_____

_____

_____

_____

What goals need improvement?

weekly
GOALS

personal

- ○
- ○
- ○
- ○

top priorities

- ☐
- ☐
- ☐

professional

- ○
- ○
- ○
- ○

top priorities

- ☐
- ☐
- ☐

spiritual

- ○
- ○
- ○
- ○

top priorities

- ☐
- ☐
- ☐

Habit Tracker

List any patterns to monitor & track good or bad habits to find work/life harmony

SUNDAY _____

MONDAY _____

TUESDAY _____

WEDNESDAY _____

THURSDAY _____

FRIDAY _____

SATURDAY _____

FITNESS TRACKER (STAY ACTIVE- EXERCISE AT LEAST 3 TIMES A WEEK, MAKE HEALTHY CHOICES, DRINK WATER

DAY	ACTIVITY	DURATION	H20
SUNDAY			
MONDAY			
TUESDAY			
WEDNESDAY			
THURSDAY			
FRIDAY			
SATURDAY			

Week of: _____ Weekly To-Do's

Monday

Tuesday

Wednesday

Thursday

Friday

Saturday & Sunday

Weekly
Inspirational Thought

_____
_____
_____
_____
_____
_____
_____
_____

Weekly
Prayer Devotion

_____
_____
_____
_____
_____

This Week's Wins:

Notes

_____
_____
_____
_____
_____
_____
_____
_____
_____
_____
_____

What goals need improvement?

weekly
GOALS

personal

- ○
- ○
- ○
- ○

top priorities

- ☐
- ☐
- ☐

professional

- ○
- ○
- ○
- ○

top priorities

- ☐
- ☐
- ☐

spiritual

- ○
- ○
- ○
- ○

top priorities

- ☐
- ☐
- ☐

Habit Tracker

List any patterns to monitor & track good or bad habits to find work/life harmony

SUNDAY _____

MONDAY _____

TUESDAY _____

WEDNESDAY _____

THURSDAY _____

FRIDAY _____

SATURDAY _____

FITNESS TRACKER (STAY ACTIVE- EXERCISE AT LEAST 3 TIMES A WEEK, MAKE HEALTHY CHOICES, DRINK WATER

DAY	ACTIVITY	DURATION	H20
SUNDAY			
MONDAY			
TUESDAY			
WEDNESDAY			
THURSDAY			
FRIDAY			
SATURDAY			

Week of: _____ Weekly To-Do's

Monday

Tuesday

Wednesday

Thursday

Friday

Saturday & Sunday

Weekly
Inspirational Thought

_____
_____
_____
_____
_____
_____
_____
_____

Weekly
Prayer Devotion

_____
_____
_____
_____
_____

This Week's Wins:

- ◯
- ◯
- ◯
- ◯

Notes

_____
_____
_____
_____
_____
_____
_____
_____
_____
_____
_____

What goals need improvement?

- ◯
- ◯
- ◯
- ◯

MONTHLY SOCIAL MEDIA PLAN

THEMES OF THE MONTH

- [ ]
- [ ]
- [ ]
- [ ]
- [ ]

BRAINSTORM POST TOPICS

_____
_____
_____
_____
_____
_____
_____
_____
_____
_____
_____

Posting Dates

Instagram	
Facebook	
Pinterest	
YouTube	
LinkedIn	

HASHTAGS/KEYWORDS

_____
_____
_____
_____
_____

NOTES

Monthly
Review

Family Time: (dinner, board games, activities, etc)

_____

_____

Maintenance Website/Update Apps:

_____

_____

Balance Financial Books

_____

_____

Cancel and/or Update Subscriptions:

_____

_____

Other:

_____

_____

MONTH-*at-a-glance*
PLANNER

MONTH:

Mon	Tues	Wed	Thur	Fri	Sat	Sun

NOTES
_____
_____
_____
_____
_____

"Don't confuse having a career with having a life." -**Gaynor Topham**

MONTHLY *expenses*

Month:_____

RECURRING EXPENSES

Software, Memberships, Household bills etc.	Amount
TOTAL RECURRING EXPENSES	$

VARIABLE EXPENSES

Contractors, Supplies, etc.	Amount
TOTAL VARIABLE EXPENSES	$
TOTAL MONTHLY EXPENSES	$

weekly
GOALS

personal

- ○
- ○
- ○
- ○

top priorities

- ☐
- ☐
- ☐

professional

- ○
- ○
- ○
- ○

top priorities

- ☐
- ☐
- ☐

spiritual

- ○
- ○
- ○
- ○

top priorities

- ☐
- ☐
- ☐

Habit Tracker

List any patterns to monitor & track good or bad habits to find work/life harmony

SUNDAY _____

MONDAY_____

TUESDAY_____

WEDNESDAY_____

THURSDAY_____

FRIDAY_____

SATURDAY_____

FITNESS TRACKER (STAY ACTIVE- EXERCISE AT LEAST 3 TIMES A WEEK, MAKE HEALTHY CHOICES, DRINK WATER

DAY	ACTIVITY	DURATION	H20
SUNDAY			
MONDAY			
TUESDAY			
WEDNESDAY			
THURSDAY			
FRIDAY			
SATURDAY			

Week of: _____ Weekly To-Do's

Monday

Tuesday

Wednesday

Thursday

Friday

Saturday & Sunday

Weekly
Inspirational Thought

_____
_____
_____
_____
_____
_____
_____

Notes

_____
_____
_____
_____
_____
_____
_____
_____
_____
_____
_____
_____

Weekly
Prayer Devotion

_____
_____
_____
_____
_____

This Week's Wins:

What goals need improvement?

weekly
GOALS

personal
- ○
- ○
- ○
- ○

top priorities
- ☐
- ☐
- ☐

professional
- ○
- ○
- ○
- ○

top priorities
- ☐
- ☐
- ☐

spiritual
- ○
- ○
- ○
- ○

top priorities
- ☐
- ☐
- ☐

Habit Tracker

List any patterns to monitor & track good or bad habits to find work/life harmony

SUNDAY _____

MONDAY _____

TUESDAY _____

WEDNESDAY _____

THURSDAY _____

FRIDAY _____

SATURDAY _____

FITNESS TRACKER (STAY ACTIVE- EXERCISE AT LEAST 3 TIMES A WEEK, MAKE HEALTHY CHOICES, DRINK WATER

DAY	ACTIVITY	DURATION	H20
SUNDAY			
MONDAY			
TUESDAY			
WEDNESDAY			
THURSDAY			
FRIDAY			
SATURDAY			

Week of: _____ Weekly To-Do's

Monday

Tuesday

Wednesday

Thursday

Friday

Saturday & Sunday

Weekly
Inspirational Thought

_____
_____
_____
_____
_____
_____
_____
_____

Weekly
Prayer Devotion

_____
_____
_____
_____
_____

Notes

_____
_____
_____
_____
_____
_____
_____
_____
_____
_____
_____

This Week's Wins:

What goals need improvement?

weekly
GOALS

personal

○

○

○

○

top priorities

☐

☐

☐

professional

○

○

○

○

top priorities

☐

☐

☐

spiritual

○

○

○

○

top priorities

☐

☐

☐

Habit Tracker

List any patterns to monitor & track good or bad habits to find work/life harmony

SUNDAY _____

MONDAY _____

TUESDAY _____

WEDNESDAY _____

THURSDAY _____

FRIDAY _____

SATURDAY _____

FITNESS TRACKER (STAY ACTIVE- EXERCISE AT LEAST 3 TIMES A WEEK, MAKE HEALTHY CHOICES, DRINK WATER

DAY	ACTIVITY	DURATION	H20
SUNDAY			
MONDAY			
TUESDAY			
WEDNESDAY			
THURSDAY			
FRIDAY			
SATURDAY			

Week of: _____ Weekly To-Do's

Monday

Tuesday

Wednesday

Thursday

Friday

Saturday & Sunday

Weekly
Inspirational Thought

_____
_____
_____
_____
_____
_____
_____
_____

Weekly
Prayer Devotion

_____
_____
_____
_____
_____

This Week's Wins:

- ⬤
- ⬤
- ⬤
- ⬤

Notes

_____
_____
_____
_____
_____
_____
_____
_____
_____
_____
_____

What goals need improvement?

- ⬤
- ⬤
- ⬤
- ⬤

weekly
GOALS

personal

- ○
- ○
- ○
- ○

top priorities

- ☐
- ☐
- ☐

professional

- ○
- ○
- ○
- ○

top priorities

- ☐
- ☐
- ☐

spiritual

- ○
- ○
- ○
- ○

top priorities

- ☐
- ☐
- ☐

Habit Tracker

List any patterns to monitor & track good or bad habits to find work/life harmony

SUNDAY _____

MONDAY _____

TUESDAY _____

WEDNESDAY _____

THURSDAY _____

FRIDAY _____

SATURDAY _____

FITNESS TRACKER (STAY ACTIVE- EXERCISE AT LEAST 3 TIMES A WEEK, MAKE HEALTHY CHOICES, DRINK WATER

DAY	ACTIVITY	DURATION	H20
SUNDAY			
MONDAY			
TUESDAY			
WEDNESDAY			
THURSDAY			
FRIDAY			
SATURDAY			

Week of: _____ Weekly To-Do's

Monday

Tuesday

Wednesday

Thursday

Friday

Saturday & Sunday

Weekly
Inspirational Thought

_____
_____
_____
_____
_____
_____
_____
_____

Weekly
Prayer Devotion

_____
_____
_____
_____
_____

This Week's Wins:

- ◯
- ◯
- ◯
- ◯

What goals need improvement?

- ◯
- ◯
- ◯
- ◯

Notes

_____
_____
_____
_____
_____
_____
_____
_____
_____
_____
_____
_____

MONTHLY SOCIAL MEDIA PLAN

Posting Dates

THEMES OF THE MONTH

☐

☐

☐

☐

☐

BRAINSTORM POST TOPICS

_____

_____

_____

_____

_____

_____

_____

_____

_____

_____

_____

HASHTAGS/KEYWORDS

_____

_____

_____

_____

_____

NOTES

Monthly
Review

Family Time: (dinner, board games, activities, etc)

_____

_____

Maintenance Website/Update Apps:

_____

_____

Balance Financial Books

_____

_____

Cancel and/or Update Subscriptions:

_____

_____

Other:

_____

_____

MONTH-*at-a-glance*
PLANNER

MONTH:

Mon	Tues	Wed	Thur	Fri	Sat	Sun

NOTES

_____

_____

_____

_____

_____

"Life is not about the quantity of things, it's about learning how to create harmony amongst what we have." -**Unknown**

MONTHLY *expenses*

Month:_____

RECURRING EXPENSES

Software, Memberships, Household bills etc.	Amount
TOTAL RECURRING EXPENSES	$

VARIABLE EXPENSES

Contractors, Supplies, etc.	Amount
TOTAL VARIABLE EXPENSES	$
TOTAL MONTHLY EXPENSES	$

weekly
GOALS

personal

- ○
- ○
- ○
- ○

top priorities

- ☐
- ☐
- ☐

professional

- ○
- ○
- ○
- ○

top priorities

- ☐
- ☐
- ☐

spiritual

- ○
- ○
- ○
- ○

top priorities

- ☐
- ☐
- ☐

Habit Tracker

List any patterns to monitor & track good or bad habits to find work/life harmony

SUNDAY _____

MONDAY _____

TUESDAY _____

WEDNESDAY _____

THURSDAY _____

FRIDAY _____

SATURDAY _____

FITNESS TRACKER (STAY ACTIVE- EXERCISE AT LEAST 3 TIMES A WEEK, MAKE HEALTHY CHOICES, DRINK WATER

DAY	ACTIVITY	DURATION	H20
SUNDAY			
MONDAY			
TUESDAY			
WEDNESDAY			
THURSDAY			
FRIDAY			
SATURDAY			

Week of: _____ Weekly To-Do's

Monday

Tuesday

Wednesday

Thursday

Friday

Saturday & Sunday

Weekly
Inspirational Thought

_____
_____
_____
_____
_____
_____
_____
_____

Weekly
Prayer Devotion

_____
_____
_____
_____
_____

This Week's Wins:

- ◯
- ◯
- ◯
- ◯

What goals need improvement?

- ◯
- ◯
- ◯
- ◯

Notes

_____
_____
_____
_____
_____
_____
_____
_____
_____
_____
_____
_____
_____

DATE:

weekly
GOALS

personal

- ○
- ○
- ○
- ○

top priorities

- ☐
- ☐
- ☐

professional

- ○
- ○
- ○
- ○

top priorities

- ☐
- ☐
- ☐

spiritual

- ○
- ○
- ○
- ○

top priorities

- ☐
- ☐
- ☐

Habit Tracker

List any patterns to monitor & track good or bad habits to find work/life harmony

SUNDAY _____

MONDAY _____

TUESDAY _____

WEDNESDAY _____

THURSDAY _____

FRIDAY _____

SATURDAY _____

FITNESS TRACKER (STAY ACTIVE- EXERCISE AT LEAST 3 TIMES A WEEK, MAKE HEALTHY CHOICES, DRINK WATER

DAY	ACTIVITY	DURATION	H20
SUNDAY			
MONDAY			
TUESDAY			
WEDNESDAY			
THURSDAY			
FRIDAY			
SATURDAY			

Week of: _____ Weekly To-Do's

Monday

Tuesday

Wednesday

Thursday

Friday

Saturday & Sunday

Weekly
Inspirational Thought

_____
_____
_____
_____
_____
_____
_____
_____
_____

Weekly
Prayer Devotion

_____
_____
_____
_____
_____

Notes

_____
_____
_____
_____
_____
_____
_____
_____
_____
_____

This Week's Wins:

- ○
- ○
- ○
- ○

What goals need improvement?

- ○
- ○
- ○
- ○

DATE: _____

weekly
GOALS

personal

- ○
- ○
- ○
- ○

top priorities

- ☐
- ☐
- ☐

professional

- ○
- ○
- ○
- ○

top priorities

- ☐
- ☐
- ☐

spiritual

- ○
- ○
- ○
- ○

top priorities

- ☐
- ☐
- ☐

Habit Tracker

List any patterns to monitor & track good or bad habits to find work/life harmony

SUNDAY _____

MONDAY_____

TUESDAY_____

WEDNESDAY_____

THURSDAY_____

FRIDAY_____

SATURDAY_____

FITNESS TRACKER (STAY ACTIVE- EXERCISE AT LEAST 3 TIMES A WEEK, MAKE HEALTHY CHOICES, DRINK WATER

DAY	ACTIVITY	DURATION	H20
SUNDAY			
MONDAY			
TUESDAY			
WEDNESDAY			
THURSDAY			
FRIDAY			
SATURDAY			

Week of: _____ Weekly To-Do's

Monday

Tuesday

Wednesday

Thursday

Friday

Saturday & Sunday

Weekly
Inspirational Thought

_____
_____
_____
_____
_____
_____
_____
_____

Weekly
Prayer Devotion

_____
_____
_____
_____
_____

This Week's Wins:

What goals need improvement?

Notes

_____
_____
_____
_____
_____
_____
_____
_____
_____
_____
_____
_____

DATE:

weekly
GOALS

personal

- ○
- ○
- ○
- ○

top priorities

- [ ]
- [ ]
- [ ]

professional

- ○
- ○
- ○
- ○

top priorities

- [ ]
- [ ]
- [ ]

spiritual

- ○
- ○
- ○
- ○

top priorities

- [ ]
- [ ]
- [ ]

Habit Tracker

List any patterns to monitor & track good or bad habits to find work/life harmony

SUNDAY _____

MONDAY _____

TUESDAY _____

WEDNESDAY _____

THURSDAY _____

FRIDAY _____

SATURDAY _____

FITNESS TRACKER (STAY ACTIVE- EXERCISE AT LEAST 3 TIMES A WEEK, MAKE HEALTHY CHOICES, DRINK WATER

DAY	ACTIVITY	DURATION	H20
SUNDAY			
MONDAY			
TUESDAY			
WEDNESDAY			
THURSDAY			
FRIDAY			
SATURDAY			

Week of: _____ Weekly To-Do's

Monday

Tuesday

Wednesday

Thursday

Friday

Saturday & Sunday

Weekly
Inspirational Thought

_____
_____
_____
_____
_____
_____
_____
_____

Weekly
Prayer Devotion

_____
_____
_____
_____
_____

Notes

_____
_____
_____
_____
_____
_____
_____
_____
_____
_____
_____
_____

This Week's Wins:

- ◯
- ◯
- ◯
- ◯

What goals need improvement?

- ◯
- ◯
- ◯
- ◯

MONTHLY SOCIAL MEDIA PLAN

THEMES OF THE MONTH

☐
☐
☐
☐
☐

Posting Dates

Instagram	
Facebook	
Pinterest	
YouTube	
LinkedIn	

BRAINSTORM POST TOPICS

_____
_____
_____
_____
_____
_____
_____
_____
_____
_____

HASHTAGS/KEYWORDS

_____
_____
_____
_____
_____
_____

NOTES

Monthly Review

Family Time: (dinner, board games, activities, etc)

_____

_____

Maintenance Website/Update Apps:

_____

_____

Balance Financial Books

_____

_____

Cancel and/or Update Subscriptions:

_____

_____

Other:

_____

_____

MONTH-*at-a-glance*
PLANNER

MONTH:

Mon	Tues	Wed	Thur	Fri	Sat	Sun

NOTES

_____

_____

_____

_____

_____

"Don't wait for the world to recognize your greatness. Live it and let the world catch up to you." -**Vincent Mafu**

MONTHLY *expenses*

Month:_____

RECURRING EXPENSES

Software, Memberships, Household bills etc.	Amount
TOTAL RECURRING EXPENSES	$

VARIABLE EXPENSES

Contractors, Supplies, etc.	Amount
TOTAL VARIABLE EXPENSES	$
TOTAL MONTHLY EXPENSES	$

DATE:

weekly
GOALS

personal

- ○
- ○
- ○
- ○

top priorities

- ☐
- ☐
- ☐

professional

- ○
- ○
- ○
- ○

top priorities

- ☐
- ☐
- ☐

spiritual

- ○
- ○
- ○
- ○

top priorities

- ☐
- ☐
- ☐

Habit Tracker

List any patterns to monitor & track good or bad habits to find work/life harmony

SUNDAY _____

MONDAY_____

TUESDAY_____

WEDNESDAY_____

THURSDAY_____

FRIDAY_____

SATURDAY_____

FITNESS TRACKER (STAY ACTIVE- EXERCISE AT LEAST 3 TIMES A WEEK, MAKE HEALTHY CHOICES, DRINK WATER

DAY	ACTIVITY	DURATION	H20
SUNDAY			
MONDAY			
TUESDAY			
WEDNESDAY			
THURSDAY			
FRIDAY			
SATURDAY			

Week of: _____ Weekly To-Do's

Monday

Tuesday

Wednesday

Thursday

Friday

Saturday & Sunday

Weekly
Inspirational Thought

_____
_____
_____
_____
_____
_____
_____
_____

Weekly
Prayer Devotion

_____
_____
_____
_____
_____

Notes

_____
_____
_____
_____
_____
_____
_____
_____
_____
_____

This Week's Wins:

What goals need improvement?

weekly
GOALS

personal

- ○
- ○
- ○
- ○

top priorities

- ☐
- ☐
- ☐

professional

- ○
- ○
- ○
- ○

top priorities

- ☐
- ☐
- ☐

spiritual

- ○
- ○
- ○
- ○

top priorities

- ☐
- ☐
- ☐

Habit Tracker

List any patterns to monitor & track good or bad habits to find work/life harmony

SUNDAY _____

MONDAY_____

TUESDAY_____

WEDNESDAY_____

THURSDAY_____

FRIDAY_____

SATURDAY_____

FITNESS TRACKER (STAY ACTIVE- EXERCISE AT LEAST 3 TIMES A WEEK, MAKE HEALTHY CHOICES, DRINK WATER

DAY	ACTIVITY	DURATION	H20
SUNDAY			
MONDAY			
TUESDAY			
WEDNESDAY			
THURSDAY			
FRIDAY			
SATURDAY			

Week of: _____ Weekly To-Do's

Monday

Tuesday

Wednesday

Thursday

Friday

Saturday & Sunday

Weekly
Inspirational Thought

_____
_____
_____
_____
_____
_____
_____
_____

Weekly
Prayer Devotion

_____
_____
_____
_____
_____

This Week's Wins:

- ◯
- ◯
- ◯
- ◯

Notes

_____
_____
_____
_____
_____
_____
_____
_____
_____
_____
_____

What goals need improvement?

- ◯
- ◯
- ◯
- ◯

weekly
GOALS

personal

- ○
- ○
- ○
- ○

top priorities

- ☐
- ☐
- ☐

professional

- ○
- ○
- ○
- ○

top priorities

- ☐
- ☐
- ☐

spiritual

- ○
- ○
- ○
- ○

top priorities

- ☐
- ☐
- ☐

Habit Tracker

List any patterns to monitor & track good or bad habits to find work/life harmony

SUNDAY _____

MONDAY_____

TUESDAY_____

WEDNESDAY_____

THURSDAY_____

FRIDAY_____

SATURDAY_____

FITNESS TRACKER (STAY ACTIVE- EXERCISE AT LEAST 3 TIMES A WEEK, MAKE HEALTHY CHOICES, DRINK WATER

DAY	ACTIVITY	DURATION	H20
SUNDAY			
MONDAY			
TUESDAY			
WEDNESDAY			
THURSDAY			
FRIDAY			
SATURDAY			

Week of: _____ Weekly To-Do's

Monday

Tuesday

Wednesday

Thursday

Friday

Saturday & Sunday

Weekly
Inspirational Thought

_____
_____
_____
_____
_____
_____
_____

Weekly
Prayer Devotion

_____
_____
_____
_____
_____

This Week's Wins:

Notes

_____
_____
_____
_____
_____
_____
_____
_____
_____
_____
_____

What goals need improvement?

DATE:

weekly
GOALS

personal

- ○
- ○
- ○
- ○

top priorities

- ☐
- ☐
- ☐

professional

- ○
- ○
- ○
- ○

top priorities

- ☐
- ☐
- ☐

spiritual

- ○
- ○
- ○
- ○

top priorities

- ☐
- ☐
- ☐

Habit Tracker

List any patterns to monitor & track good or bad habits to find work/life harmony

SUNDAY _____

MONDAY _____

TUESDAY _____

WEDNESDAY _____

THURSDAY _____

FRIDAY _____

SATURDAY _____

FITNESS TRACKER (STAY ACTIVE- EXERCISE AT LEAST 3 TIMES A WEEK, MAKE HEALTHY CHOICES, DRINK WATER

DAY	ACTIVITY	DURATION	H20
SUNDAY			
MONDAY			
TUESDAY			
WEDNESDAY			
THURSDAY			
FRIDAY			
SATURDAY			

Week of: _____ Weekly To-Do's

Monday

Tuesday

Wednesday

Thursday

Friday

Saturday & Sunday

Weekly
Inspirational Thought

_____
_____
_____
_____
_____
_____
_____
_____

Notes

_____
_____
_____
_____
_____
_____
_____
_____
_____
_____
_____
_____

Weekly
Prayer Devotion

_____
_____
_____
_____
_____

This Week's Wins:

- ◯
- ◯
- ◯
- ◯

What goals need improvement?

- ◯
- ◯
- ◯
- ◯

MONTHLY SOCIAL MEDIA PLAN

THEMES OF THE MONTH

☐

☐

☐

☐

☐

BRAINSTORM POST TOPICS

_____

_____

_____

_____

_____

_____

_____

_____

_____

_____

_____

Posting Dates

Instagram	
Facebook	
Pinterest	
YouTube	
LinkedIn	

HASHTAGS/KEYWORDS

_____

_____

_____

_____

_____

NOTES

Monthly
Review

Family Time: (dinner, board games, activities, etc)

_____

_____

Maintenance Website/Update Apps:

_____

_____

Balance Financial Books

_____

_____

Cancel and/or Update Subscriptions:

_____

_____

Other:

_____

_____

MONTH-*at-a-glance*
PLANNER

MONTH:

Mon	Tues	Wed	Thur	Fri	Sat	Sun

NOTES

_____
_____
_____
_____
_____

"Every day may not be good, but there's something good in every day."
-Alice Morse Earle

MONTHLY *expenses*

Month:_____

RECURRING EXPENSES

Software, Memberships, Household bills etc.	Amount
TOTAL RECURRING EXPENSES	$

VARIABLE EXPENSES

Contractors, Supplies, etc.	Amount
TOTAL VARIABLE EXPENSES	$

| **TOTAL MONTHLY EXPENSES** | $ |

DATE:

weekly
GOALS

personal

- ○
- ○
- ○
- ○

top priorities

- ☐
- ☐
- ☐

professional

- ○
- ○
- ○
- ○

top priorities

- ☐
- ☐
- ☐

spiritual

- ○
- ○
- ○
- ○

top priorities

- ☐
- ☐
- ☐

Habit Tracker

List any patterns to monitor & track good or bad habits to find work/life harmony

SUNDAY _____

MONDAY _____

TUESDAY _____

WEDNESDAY _____

THURSDAY _____

FRIDAY _____

SATURDAY _____

FITNESS TRACKER (STAY ACTIVE- EXERCISE AT LEAST 3 TIMES A WEEK, MAKE HEALTHY CHOICES, DRINK WATER

DAY	ACTIVITY	DURATION	H20
SUNDAY			
MONDAY			
TUESDAY			
WEDNESDAY			
THURSDAY			
FRIDAY			
SATURDAY			

Week of: _____ Weekly To-Do's

Monday

Tuesday

Wednesday

Thursday

Friday

Saturday & Sunday

Weekly
Inspirational Thought

_____
_____
_____
_____
_____
_____
_____
_____

Weekly
Prayer Devotion

_____
_____
_____
_____
_____

This Week's Wins:

- ◯
- ◯
- ◯
- ◯

What goals need improvement?

- ◯
- ◯
- ◯
- ◯

Notes

_____
_____
_____
_____
_____
_____
_____
_____
_____
_____
_____
_____

weekly
GOALS

personal

- ○
- ○
- ○
- ○

top priorities

- ☐
- ☐
- ☐

professional

- ○
- ○
- ○
- ○

top priorities

- ☐
- ☐
- ☐

spiritual

- ○
- ○
- ○
- ○

top priorities

- ☐
- ☐
- ☐

Habit Tracker

List any patterns to monitor & track good or bad habits to find work/life harmony

SUNDAY _____

MONDAY _____

TUESDAY _____

WEDNESDAY _____

THURSDAY _____

FRIDAY _____

SATURDAY _____

FITNESS TRACKER (STAY ACTIVE- EXERCISE AT LEAST 3 TIMES A WEEK, MAKE HEALTHY CHOICES, DRINK WATER

DAY	ACTIVITY	DURATION	H20
SUNDAY			
MONDAY			
TUESDAY			
WEDNESDAY			
THURSDAY			
FRIDAY			
SATURDAY			

Week of: _____ Weekly To-Do's

Monday

Tuesday

Wednesday

Thursday

Friday

Saturday & Sunday

Weekly
Inspirational Thought

_____
_____
_____
_____
_____
_____
_____
_____

Weekly
Prayer Devotion

_____
_____
_____
_____
_____

This Week's Wins:

What goals need improvement?

Notes

_____
_____
_____
_____
_____
_____
_____
_____
_____
_____

weekly
GOALS

personal

- ○
- ○
- ○
- ○

top priorities

- ☐
- ☐
- ☐

professional

- ○
- ○
- ○
- ○

top priorities

- ☐
- ☐
- ☐

spiritual

- ○
- ○
- ○
- ○

top priorities

- ☐
- ☐
- ☐

Habit Tracker

List any patterns to monitor & track good or bad habits to find work/life harmony

SUNDAY _____

MONDAY _____

TUESDAY _____

WEDNESDAY _____

THURSDAY _____

FRIDAY _____

SATURDAY _____

FITNESS TRACKER (STAY ACTIVE- EXERCISE AT LEAST 3 TIMES A WEEK, MAKE HEALTHY CHOICES, DRINK WATER

DAY	ACTIVITY	DURATION	H20
SUNDAY			
MONDAY			
TUESDAY			
WEDNESDAY			
THURSDAY			
FRIDAY			
SATURDAY			

Week of: _____ Weekly To-Do's

Monday

Tuesday

Wednesday

Thursday

Friday

Saturday & Sunday

Weekly
Inspirational Thought

_____
_____
_____
_____
_____
_____
_____
_____

Weekly
Prayer Devotion

_____
_____
_____
_____
_____

This Week's Wins:

Notes

_____
_____
_____
_____
_____
_____
_____
_____
_____
_____
_____

What goals need improvement?

DATE:

weekly
GOALS

personal
- ○
- ○
- ○
- ○

top priorities
- ☐
- ☐
- ☐

professional
- ○
- ○
- ○
- ○

top priorities
- ☐
- ☐
- ☐

spiritual
- ○
- ○
- ○
- ○

top priorities
- ☐
- ☐
- ☐

Habit Tracker

List any patterns to monitor & track good or bad habits to find work/life harmony

SUNDAY _____

MONDAY _____

TUESDAY _____

WEDNESDAY _____

THURSDAY _____

FRIDAY _____

SATURDAY _____

FITNESS TRACKER (STAY ACTIVE- EXERCISE AT LEAST 3 TIMES A WEEK, MAKE HEALTHY CHOICES, DRINK WATER

DAY	ACTIVITY	DURATION	H20
SUNDAY			
MONDAY			
TUESDAY			
WEDNESDAY			
THURSDAY			
FRIDAY			
SATURDAY			

Week of: _____ Weekly To-Do's

Monday

Tuesday

Wednesday

Thursday

Friday

Saturday & Sunday

Weekly
Inspirational Thought

_____
_____
_____
_____
_____
_____
_____
_____

Weekly
Prayer Devotion

_____
_____
_____
_____
_____

This Week's Wins:

- ◯
- ◯
- ◯
- ◯

Notes

_____
_____
_____
_____
_____
_____
_____
_____
_____
_____
_____
_____

What goals need improvement?

- ◯
- ◯
- ◯
- ◯

MONTHLY SOCIAL MEDIA PLAN

THEMES OF THE MONTH

- [ ]
- [ ]
- [ ]
- [ ]
- [ ]

BRAINSTORM POST TOPICS

_____
_____
_____
_____
_____
_____
_____
_____
_____
_____

Posting Dates

Instagram	
Facebook	
Pinterest	
YouTube	
LinkedIn	

HASHTAGS/KEYWORDS

_____
_____
_____
_____
_____

NOTES

Monthly Review

Family Time: (dinner, board games, activities, etc)

_____

_____

Maintenance Website/Update Apps:

_____

_____

Balance Financial Books

_____

_____

Cancel and/or Update Subscriptions:

_____

_____

Other:

_____

_____

MONTH-*at-a-glance*
PLANNER

MONTH:

Mon	Tues	Wed	Thur	Fri	Sat	Sun

NOTES

_____

_____

_____

_____

_____

"A Kind word, a genuine smile, a selfless act can make a difference in someone's day. Will today be that day?" - **Caroline Naoroji**

MONTHLY *expenses*

Month:_____

RECURRING EXPENSES	
Software, Memberships, Household bills etc.	Amount
TOTAL RECURRING EXPENSES	$

VARIABLE EXPENSES	
Contractors, Supplies, etc.	Amount
TOTAL VARIABLE EXPENSES	$

TOTAL MONTHLY EXPENSES	$

DATE:

weekly
GOALS

personal

- ○
- ○
- ○
- ○

top priorities

- ☐
- ☐
- ☐

professional

- ○
- ○
- ○
- ○

top priorities

- ☐
- ☐
- ☐

spiritual

- ○
- ○
- ○
- ○

top priorities

- ☐
- ☐
- ☐

Habit Tracker

List any patterns to monitor & track good or bad habits to find work/life harmony

SUNDAY _____

MONDAY _____

TUESDAY _____

WEDNESDAY _____

THURSDAY _____

FRIDAY _____

SATURDAY _____

FITNESS TRACKER (STAY ACTIVE- EXERCISE AT LEAST 3 TIMES A WEEK, MAKE HEALTHY CHOICES, DRINK WATER

DAY	ACTIVITY	DURATION	H20
SUNDAY			
MONDAY			
TUESDAY			
WEDNESDAY			
THURSDAY			
FRIDAY			
SATURDAY			

Week of: _____ Weekly To-Do's

Monday

Tuesday

Wednesday

Thursday

Friday

Saturday & Sunday

Weekly
Inspirational Thought

_____
_____
_____
_____
_____
_____
_____
_____

Weekly
Prayer Devotion

_____
_____
_____
_____
_____

This Week's Wins:

- ○
- ○
- ○
- ○

What goals need improvement?

- ○
- ○
- ○
- ○

Notes

_____
_____
_____
_____
_____
_____
_____
_____
_____
_____
_____

DATE:

weekly
GOALS

personal
- ○
- ○
- ○
- ○

top priorities
- ☐
- ☐
- ☐

professional
- ○
- ○
- ○
- ○

top priorities
- ☐
- ☐
- ☐

spiritual
- ○
- ○
- ○
- ○

top priorities
- ☐
- ☐
- ☐

Habit Tracker

List any patterns to monitor & track good or bad habits to find work/life harmony

SUNDAY _____

MONDAY _____

TUESDAY _____

WEDNESDAY _____

THURSDAY _____

FRIDAY _____

SATURDAY _____

FITNESS TRACKER (STAY ACTIVE- EXERCISE AT LEAST 3 TIMES A WEEK, MAKE HEALTHY CHOICES, DRINK WATER

DAY	ACTIVITY	DURATION	H20
SUNDAY			
MONDAY			
TUESDAY			
WEDNESDAY			
THURSDAY			
FRIDAY			
SATURDAY			

Week of: _____ Weekly To-Do's

Monday

Tuesday

Wednesday

Thursday

Friday

Saturday & Sunday

Weekly
Inspirational Thought

_____

_____

_____

_____

_____

_____

_____

Weekly
Prayer Devotion

_____

_____

_____

_____

_____

This Week's Wins:

Notes

_____

_____

_____

_____

_____

_____

_____

_____

_____

_____

_____

_____

What goals need improvement?

DATE:

weekly
GOALS

personal

- ○
- ○
- ○
- ○

top priorities

- ☐
- ☐
- ☐

professional

- ○
- ○
- ○
- ○

top priorities

- ☐
- ☐
- ☐

spiritual

- ○
- ○
- ○
- ○

top priorities

- ☐
- ☐
- ☐

Habit Tracker

List any patterns to monitor & track good or bad habits to find work/life harmony

SUNDAY _____

MONDAY _____

TUESDAY _____

WEDNESDAY _____

THURSDAY _____

FRIDAY _____

SATURDAY _____

FITNESS TRACKER (STAY ACTIVE- EXERCISE AT LEAST 3 TIMES A WEEK, MAKE HEALTHY CHOICES, DRINK WATER

DAY	ACTIVITY	DURATION	H20
SUNDAY			
MONDAY			
TUESDAY			
WEDNESDAY			
THURSDAY			
FRIDAY			
SATURDAY			

Week of: _____ Weekly To-Do's

Monday

Tuesday

Wednesday

Thursday

Friday

Saturday & Sunday

Weekly
Inspirational Thought

_____
_____
_____
_____
_____
_____
_____
_____

Weekly
Prayer Devotion

_____
_____
_____
_____
_____

This Week's Wins:

Notes

_____
_____
_____
_____
_____
_____
_____
_____
_____
_____
_____
_____
_____

What goals need improvement?

DATE:

weekly
GOALS

personal

- ○
- ○
- ○
- ○

top priorities

- ☐
- ☐
- ☐

professional

- ○
- ○
- ○
- ○

top priorities

- ☐
- ☐
- ☐

spiritual

- ○
- ○
- ○
- ○

top priorities

- ☐
- ☐
- ☐

Habit Tracker

List any patterns to monitor & track good or bad habits to find work/life harmony

SUNDAY _____

MONDAY _____

TUESDAY _____

WEDNESDAY _____

THURSDAY _____

FRIDAY _____

SATURDAY _____

FITNESS TRACKER (STAY ACTIVE- EXERCISE AT LEAST 3 TIMES A WEEK, MAKE HEALTHY CHOICES, DRINK WATER

DAY	ACTIVITY	DURATION	H20
SUNDAY			
MONDAY			
TUESDAY			
WEDNESDAY			
THURSDAY			
FRIDAY			
SATURDAY			

Week of: _____ Weekly To-Do's

Monday

Tuesday

Wednesday

Thursday

Friday

Saturday & Sunday

Weekly
Inspirational Thought

_____
_____
_____
_____
_____
_____
_____

Weekly
Prayer Devotion

_____
_____
_____
_____
_____

This Week's Wins:

- ○
- ○
- ○
- ○

What goals need improvement?

- ○
- ○
- ○
- ○

Notes

_____
_____
_____
_____
_____
_____
_____
_____
_____
_____
_____
_____

MONTHLY SOCIAL MEDIA PLAN

THEMES OF THE MONTH

- [ ]
- [ ]
- [ ]
- [ ]
- [ ]

BRAINSTORM POST TOPICS

Posting Dates

Instagram	
Facebook	
Pinterest	
YouTube	
LinkedIn	

HASHTAGS/KEYWORDS

NOTES

Monthly
Review

Family Time: (dinner, board games, activities, etc)

_____

_____

Maintenance Website/Update Apps:

_____

_____

Balance Financial Books

_____

_____

Cancel and/or Update Subscriptions:

_____

_____

Other:

_____

_____

MONTH-*at-a-glance*
PLANNER

MONTH:

Mon	Tues	Wed	Thur	Fri	Sat	Sun

NOTES

_____

_____

_____   *"A better life starts with the*

_____   *transformation in your mind." -*

_____   **Unknown**

MONTHLY *expenses*

Month:_____

RECURRING EXPENSES

Software, Memberships, Household bills etc.	Amount
TOTAL RECURRING EXPENSES	$

VARIABLE EXPENSES

Contractors, Supplies, etc.	Amount
TOTAL VARIABLE EXPENSES	$
TOTAL MONTHLY EXPENSES	$

DATE:

weekly
GOALS

personal

- ○
- ○
- ○
- ○

top priorities

- ☐
- ☐
- ☐

professional

- ○
- ○
- ○
- ○

top priorities

- ☐
- ☐
- ☐

spiritual

- ○
- ○
- ○
- ○

top priorities

- ☐
- ☐
- ☐

Habit Tracker

List any patterns to monitor & track good or bad habits to find work/life harmony

SUNDAY _____

MONDAY _____

TUESDAY _____

WEDNESDAY _____

THURSDAY _____

FRIDAY _____

SATURDAY _____

FITNESS TRACKER (STAY ACTIVE- EXERCISE AT LEAST 3 TIMES A WEEK, MAKE HEALTHY CHOICES, DRINK WATER

DAY	ACTIVITY	DURATION	H20
SUNDAY			
MONDAY			
TUESDAY			
WEDNESDAY			
THURSDAY			
FRIDAY			
SATURDAY			

Week of: _____ Weekly To-Do's

Monday

Tuesday

Wednesday

Thursday

Friday

Saturday & Sunday

Weekly
Inspirational Thought

_____
_____
_____
_____
_____
_____
_____

Weekly
Prayer Devotion

_____
_____
_____
_____
_____

This Week's Wins:

- ⬜
- ⬜
- ⬜
- ⬜

Notes

_____
_____
_____
_____
_____
_____
_____
_____
_____
_____

What goals need improvement?

- ⬜
- ⬜
- ⬜
- ⬜

weekly
GOALS

personal

- ○
- ○
- ○
- ○

top priorities

- ☐
- ☐
- ☐

professional

- ○
- ○
- ○
- ○

top priorities

- ☐
- ☐
- ☐

spiritual

- ○
- ○
- ○
- ○

top priorities

- ☐
- ☐
- ☐

Habit Tracker

List any patterns to monitor & track good or bad habits to find work/life harmony

SUNDAY _____

MONDAY _____

TUESDAY _____

WEDNESDAY _____

THURSDAY _____

FRIDAY _____

SATURDAY _____

FITNESS TRACKER (STAY ACTIVE- EXERCISE AT LEAST 3 TIMES A WEEK, MAKE HEALTHY CHOICES, DRINK WATER

DAY	ACTIVITY	DURATION	H20
SUNDAY			
MONDAY			
TUESDAY			
WEDNESDAY			
THURSDAY			
FRIDAY			
SATURDAY			

Week of: _____ Weekly To-Do's

Monday

Tuesday

Wednesday

Thursday

Friday

Saturday & Sunday

Weekly
Inspirational Thought

_____
_____
_____
_____
_____
_____
_____

Notes

_____
_____
_____
_____
_____
_____
_____
_____
_____
_____
_____

Weekly
Prayer Devotion

_____
_____
_____
_____

This Week's Wins:

- ◯
- ◯
- ◯
- ◯

What goals need improvement?

- ◯
- ◯
- ◯
- ◯

DATE:

weekly
GOALS

personal

- ○
- ○
- ○
- ○

top priorities

- ☐
- ☐
- ☐

professional

- ○
- ○
- ○
- ○

top priorities

- ☐
- ☐
- ☐

spiritual

- ○
- ○
- ○
- ○

top priorities

- ☐
- ☐
- ☐

Habit Tracker

List any patterns to monitor & track good or bad habits to find work/life harmony

SUNDAY _____

MONDAY _____

TUESDAY _____

WEDNESDAY _____

THURSDAY _____

FRIDAY _____

SATURDAY _____

FITNESS TRACKER (STAY ACTIVE- EXERCISE AT LEAST 3 TIMES A WEEK, MAKE HEALTHY CHOICES, DRINK WATER

DAY	ACTIVITY	DURATION	H20
SUNDAY			
MONDAY			
TUESDAY			
WEDNESDAY			
THURSDAY			
FRIDAY			
SATURDAY			

Week of: _____ Weekly To-Do's

Monday

Tuesday

Wednesday

Thursday

Friday

Saturday & Sunday

Weekly
Inspirational Thought

_____
_____
_____
_____
_____
_____
_____
_____
_____

Weekly
Prayer Devotion

_____
_____
_____
_____
_____

This Week's Wins:

What goals need improvement?

Notes

_____
_____
_____
_____
_____
_____
_____
_____
_____
_____
_____

weekly
GOALS

personal

- ○
- ○
- ○
- ○

top priorities

- ☐
- ☐
- ☐

professional

- ○
- ○
- ○
- ○

top priorities

- ☐
- ☐
- ☐

spiritual

- ○
- ○
- ○
- ○

top priorities

- ☐
- ☐
- ☐

Habit Tracker

List any patterns to monitor & track good or bad habits to find work/life harmony

SUNDAY _____

MONDAY _____

TUESDAY _____

WEDNESDAY _____

THURSDAY _____

FRIDAY _____

SATURDAY _____

FITNESS TRACKER (STAY ACTIVE- EXERCISE AT LEAST 3 TIMES A WEEK, MAKE HEALTHY CHOICES, DRINK WATER

DAY	ACTIVITY	DURATION	H20
SUNDAY			
MONDAY			
TUESDAY			
WEDNESDAY			
THURSDAY			
FRIDAY			
SATURDAY			

Week of: _____ Weekly To-Do's

Monday

Tuesday

Wednesday

Thursday

Friday

Saturday & Sunday

Weekly
Inspirational Thought

_____

_____

_____

_____

_____

_____

_____

_____

_____

Notes

_____

_____

_____

_____

_____

_____

_____

_____

_____

_____

_____

_____

Weekly
Prayer Devotion

_____

_____

_____

_____

_____

This Week's Wins:

What goals need improvement?

MONTHLY SOCIAL MEDIA PLAN

THEMES OF THE MONTH

- [ ]
- [ ]
- [ ]
- [ ]
- [ ]

BRAINSTORM POST TOPICS

Posting Dates

Instagram	
Facebook	
Pinterest	
YouTube	
LinkedIn	

HASHTAGS/KEYWORDS

NOTES

Monthly Review

Family Time: (dinner, board games, activities, etc)

_____

_____

Maintenance Website/Update Apps:

_____

_____

Balance Financial Books

_____

_____

Cancel and/or Update Subscriptions:

_____

_____

Other:

_____

_____

MONTH-*at-a-glance* PLANNER

MONTH:

Mon	Tues	Wed	Thur	Fri	Sat	Sun

NOTES

_____

_____

_____   *"Life is what happens when you're*

_____   *busy making other plans."* -**John**

_____   **Lennon**

MONTHLY *expenses*

Month:_____

RECURRING EXPENSES

Software, Memberships, Household bills etc.	Amount
TOTAL RECURRING EXPENSES	$

VARIABLE EXPENSES

Contractors, Supplies, etc.	Amount
TOTAL VARIABLE EXPENSES	$
TOTAL MONTHLY EXPENSES	$

DATE: _____

weekly
GOALS

personal

○

○

○

○

top priorities

☐

☐

☐

professional

○

○

○

○

top priorities

☐

☐

☐

spiritual

○

○

○

○

top priorities

☐

☐

☐

Habit Tracker

List any patterns to monitor & track good or bad habits to find work/life harmony

SUNDAY _____

MONDAY_____

TUESDAY_____

WEDNESDAY_____

THURSDAY_____

FRIDAY_____

SATURDAY_____

FITNESS TRACKER (STAY ACTIVE- EXERCISE AT LEAST 3 TIMES A WEEK, MAKE HEALTHY CHOICES, DRINK WATER

DAY	ACTIVITY	DURATION	H20
SUNDAY			
MONDAY			
TUESDAY			
WEDNESDAY			
THURSDAY			
FRIDAY			
SATURDAY			

Week of: _____ Weekly To-Do's

Monday

Tuesday

Wednesday

Thursday

Friday

Saturday & Sunday

Weekly
Inspirational Thought

_____
_____
_____
_____
_____
_____
_____
_____

Weekly
Prayer Devotion

_____
_____
_____
_____
_____

This Week's Wins:

Notes

_____
_____
_____
_____
_____
_____
_____
_____
_____
_____
_____
_____

What goals need improvement?

DATE: _____

weekly
GOALS

personal

○

○

○

○

top priorities

☐

☐

☐

professional

○

○

○

○

top priorities

☐

☐

☐

spiritual

○

○

○

○

top priorities

☐

☐

☐

Habit Tracker

List any patterns to monitor & track good or bad habits to find work/life harmony

SUNDAY _____

MONDAY_____

TUESDAY_____

WEDNESDAY_____

THURSDAY_____

FRIDAY_____

SATURDAY_____

FITNESS TRACKER (STAY ACTIVE- EXERCISE AT LEAST 3 TIMES A WEEK, MAKE HEALTHY CHOICES, DRINK WATER

DAY	ACTIVITY	DURATION	H20
SUNDAY			
MONDAY			
TUESDAY			
WEDNESDAY			
THURSDAY			
FRIDAY			
SATURDAY			

Week of: _____ Weekly To-Do's

Monday

Tuesday

Wednesday

Thursday

Friday

Saturday & Sunday

Weekly
Inspirational Thought

_____

_____

_____

_____

_____

_____

_____

_____

Weekly
Prayer Devotion

_____

_____

_____

_____

_____

This Week's Wins:

- ○
- ○
- ○
- ○

What goals need improvement?

- ○
- ○
- ○
- ○

Notes

_____

_____

_____

_____

_____

_____

_____

_____

_____

_____

_____

DATE:
_____

weekly
GOALS

personal

- ○
- ○
- ○
- ○

top priorities

- ☐
- ☐
- ☐

professional

- ○
- ○
- ○
- ○

top priorities

- ☐
- ☐
- ☐

spiritual

- ○
- ○
- ○
- ○

top priorities

- ☐
- ☐
- ☐

Habit Tracker

List any patterns to monitor & track good or bad habits to find work/life harmony

SUNDAY _____

MONDAY _____

TUESDAY _____

WEDNESDAY _____

THURSDAY _____

FRIDAY _____

SATURDAY _____

FITNESS TRACKER (STAY ACTIVE- EXERCISE AT LEAST 3 TIMES A WEEK, MAKE HEALTHY CHOICES, DRINK WATER

DAY	ACTIVITY	DURATION	H20
SUNDAY			
MONDAY			
TUESDAY			
WEDNESDAY			
THURSDAY			
FRIDAY			
SATURDAY			

Week of: _____ Weekly To-Do's

Monday

Tuesday

Wednesday

Thursday

Friday

Saturday & Sunday

Weekly
Inspirational Thought

_____
_____
_____
_____
_____
_____
_____

Weekly
Prayer Devotion

_____
_____
_____
_____
_____

This Week's Wins:

- ○
- ○
- ○
- ○

What goals need improvement?

- ○
- ○
- ○
- ○

Notes

_____
_____
_____
_____
_____
_____
_____
_____
_____
_____
_____
_____

DATE:

weekly
GOALS

personal

- ○
- ○
- ○
- ○

top priorities

- ☐
- ☐
- ☐

professional

- ○
- ○
- ○
- ○

top priorities

- ☐
- ☐
- ☐

spiritual

- ○
- ○
- ○
- ○

top priorities

- ☐
- ☐
- ☐

Habit Tracker

List any patterns to monitor & track good or bad habits to find work/life harmony

SUNDAY _____

MONDAY _____

TUESDAY _____

WEDNESDAY _____

THURSDAY _____

FRIDAY _____

SATURDAY _____

FITNESS TRACKER (STAY ACTIVE- EXERCISE AT LEAST 3 TIMES A WEEK, MAKE HEALTHY CHOICES, DRINK WATER

DAY	ACTIVITY	DURATION	H20
SUNDAY			
MONDAY			
TUESDAY			
WEDNESDAY			
THURSDAY			
FRIDAY			
SATURDAY			

Week of: _____ Weekly To-Do's

Monday

Tuesday

Wednesday

Thursday

Friday

Saturday & Sunday

Weekly
Inspirational Thought

_____
_____
_____
_____
_____
_____
_____
_____

Notes

_____
_____
_____
_____
_____
_____
_____
_____
_____
_____
_____
_____

Weekly
Prayer Devotion

_____
_____
_____
_____
_____

This Week's Wins:

What goals need improvement?

MONTHLY SOCIAL MEDIA PLAN

THEMES OF THE MONTH

- [ ]
- [ ]
- [ ]
- [ ]
- [ ]

BRAINSTORM POST TOPICS

_____
_____
_____
_____
_____
_____
_____
_____
_____
_____

Posting Dates

Instagram	
Facebook	
Pinterest	
YouTube	
LinkedIn	

HASHTAGS/KEYWORDS

_____
_____
_____
_____
_____
_____

NOTES

Monthly Review

Family Time: (dinner, board games, activities, etc)

_____

_____

Maintenance Website/Update Apps:

_____

_____

Balance Financial Books

_____

_____

Cancel and/or Update Subscriptions:

_____

_____

Other:

_____

_____

MONTHLY INCOME *Tracker*

JANUARY
Total $

Notes

FEBRUARY
Total $

Notes

MARCH
Total $

Notes

APRIL
Total $

Notes

MAY
Total $

Notes

JUNE
Total $

Notes

JULY
Total $

Notes

AUGUST
Total $

Notes

SEPTEMBER
Total $

Notes

OCTOBER
Total $

Notes

NOVEMBER
Total $

Notes

DECEMBER
Total $

Notes

Printed in the USA
CPSIA information can be obtained
at www.ICGtesting.com
LVHW060239210224
772377LV00073B/2549

9 781955 605458